ALWAYS GIVE UP!

DISCLAIMER

THIS BOOK IS NOT A CALENDAR. IT DOES NOT CONTAIN DAYS OF THE WEEK. IT CAN BE USED IN ANY YEAR, ANYTIME.

THIS BOOK WAS CREATED WITH THE INTENT TO ENTERTAIN.

THIS MANUAL IS INTENDED TO BE A PARODY OF ALL THE PERSONAL GROWTH MANUALS OUT THERE.

THE AUTHOR REFRAINS FROM REGARDING THE ADVICE GIVEN IN THIS MANUAL AS SINCERE ADVICE SINCE THIS BOOK IS INTENDED TO BE IRONIC.

SO PLEASE, READ THE BOOK AS IT IS INTENDED TO BE READ.

I DIDN'T KNOW
HOW TO REMOVE
THESE EDGES SO I
GAVE UP AND LEFT
THEM THERE
(ALWAYS GIVE UP)

JAN 1

DO YOU REALLY THINK THIS YEAR WILL BE BETTER?

IT WON'T.

IT WON'T

JAN 2

PRIORITIZE BAD IDEAS OVER GOOD ONES.

JAN 3

IF YOU THINK YOU ARE A LOSER.

AT LEAST YOU ARE RIGHT ABOUT SOMETHING.

JAN 4

PLEASE STOP TRUST YOURSELF.

JAN 5

ALWAYS GIVE UP.

JAN 6

IS THIS THE BEST YOU CAN DO?

I BET YOU CAN DO A LOT WORSE.

JAN 7

STOP WANDERING IF YOU'RE GOOD ENOUGH.

'CAUSE YOU'RE NOT.

JAN 8

EVERYTHING IS GOING TO BE OK.

BUT NOT TODAY.

JAN 9

EMPHASIZES THE THINGS THAT DON'T MATTER.

JAN 10

IF NOT TODAY, WHEN?

MAKE NOW YOUR WRONG DECISION.

JAN 11

TIRED OF YOUR JOB?

KEEP GOING. IT WILL GET WORSE.

JAN 12

NO ONE WILL HELP YOU.

YOU SHOULD BE THE ADULT NOW.

JAN 13

STOP WONDERING.

YES, IT'S JUST YOUR FAULT

JAN 14

PROCRASTINATING IS BETTER THAN ACTING.

JAN 15

DON'T BE THE CHANGE YOU WANT TO SEE IN THE WORLD.

LET OTHERS DO SOMETHING.

JAN 16

YOU' RE NOT SPECIAL.

JAN 17

DON'T EXPECT TOO MUCH

BECAUSE IT WON'T HAPPEN.

JAN 18

IT'S BETTER IF YOU COMPLAIN BECAUSE DOING SOMETHING WON'T HELP.

JAN 19

THE BEST THING TO DO IS NOT EVEN TRY.

JAN 20

IF YOU THINK OTHERS ARE DOING BETTER THAN YOU, YOU MAY BE RIGHT.

JAN 21

DON'T LET OTHERS BURST YOU DOWN.

DO IT YOURSELF.

JAN 22

AMBITION IS THE FIRST STEP TOWARDS DISAPPOINTMENT.

JAN 23

RELAX.

YOU ARE NOT GOING TO CHANGE THE WORLD.

JAN 24

DON'T PUT YOUR THOUGHTS IN PLACE.

KEEP LIVING IN THIS MESS.

JAN 25

DON' T LET OTHERS THINK YOU ARE A LOSER.

PROVE IT TO THEM.

JAN 26

MAKE PEOPLE BORED AS THEY LISTEN TO YOU.

JAN 27

NO MATTER HOW MANY TIMES YOU TRY.

YOU WILL ALWAYS FAIL.

JAN 28

WHY TRY YOUR BEST WHEN MEDIOCRITY IS SO MUCH EASIER?

JAN 29

YOU' RE NOT ENOUGH.

JAN 30

IF YOU MAKE A MISTAKE, YOU WON'T GET A SECOND CHANCE.

JAN 31

PROCRASTINATION: BECAUSE EVENTUALLY IS GOOD ENOUGH.

FEB 1

YOU ARE WORSE THAN YOU THINK.

FEB 2

THERE IS NO SHAME IN FAILURE.

NOT ALWAYS.

SOMETIMES IT'S BETTER TO BE ASHAMED.

FEB 3

WHY DO YOU TRY SO HARD?

IT'S USELESS AND YOU KNOW IT.

FEB 4

EFFORT IS JUST A WAY TO PROLONG THE INEVITABLE DISAPPOINTMENT.

FEB 5

NO ONE CARES ABOUT WHAT YOU DO.

FEB 6

KEEP OVERTHINKING.

IT'S GOOD FOR YOUR MENTAL HEALTH.

FEB 7

IT'S FUNNY HOW YOU'RE STILL HOPING THAT A GREAT OPPORTUNITY WILL ARRIVE.

FEB 8

NO ONE CARES ABOUT YOUR PROBLEMS.

FEB 9

WHY AIM FOR THE STARS WHEN YOU CAN COMFORTABLY STAY IN THE GUTTER?

FEB 10

IF AT FIRST YOU DON'T SUCCEED, CONSIDER IT A SIGN TO STOP TRYING.

FEB 11

TRY HARDER.

TO MAKE THE FAILURE
MORE PAINFUL.

FEB 12

YES, IT'S ONLY YOUR FAULT.

FEB 13

TODAY YOU ARE NOT THE SAME PERSON YOU WERE YESTERDAY.

TODAY YOU ARE MORE TIRED AND WEAKER.

FEB 14

BUILD TOXIC RELATIONSHIPS.

FEB 15

FIND A HOBBY THAT WILL MAKE YOU WASTE YOUR TIME.

FEB 16

DON'T MAKE THE MOST OF TODAY.

FEB 17

QUICK TIP:

DO NOTHING WHILE FEELING BAD ABOUT DOING NOTHING.

FEB 18

DON'T DO TODAY WHAT YOU MIGHT DO TOMORROW.

FEB 19

GYM SUBSCRIPTION CAN WAIT ANOTHER WEEK.

FEB 20

WANT SOMETHING FUNNY?

REMEMBER WHEN YOU THOUGHT YOU WERE GOING TO MAKE IT.

FEB 21

YOU HAVE NOT YET MEET THE PERSON WHO WILL MAKE YOU FEEL LIKE A REAL FAILURE.

FEB 22

KARMA DOES NOT EXIST.
IF IT GOES WRONG NOW, IT WILL CONTINUE TO GO WRONG IN THE FUTURE.

FEB 23

INSPIRATION IS FLEETING, BUT MEDIOCRITY LASTS FOREVER.

FEB 24

AMBITION IS THE PATH TO DISAPPOINTMENT; MEDIOCRITY IS THE ROAD TO CONTENTMENT.

FEB 25

DON'T OPEN YOUR MIND.

FEB 26

BELIEVE WHAT YOU SEE ON SOCIAL NETWORKS.

IT'S ALL TRUE.

FEB 27

THE ONLY PERSON YOU CAN TRURLY RELY ON IS YOU.

THAT'S THE ISSUE.

FEB 28

STOP REMEMBERING THE PAST.

IT WAS A MESS AS MUCH AS THE PRESENT.

FEB 29

IF THIS DAY DOES NOT EXIST, USE THIS PAGE TO WIPE AWAY YOUR TEARS.

YOU NEED IT.

MAR 1

TODAY YOU SHOULD CRY FOR NO REASON.

MAR 2

TODAY IS NOT SO BAD COMPARED TO THE DAYS TO COME.

MAR 3

DO NOT EXPRESS YOUR FEELINGS TO ANYONE. AVOID THIS EMBARRASSMENT.

MAR 4

WHY SET HIGH EXPECTATIONS WHEN LOW ONES ARE SO MUCH EASIER TO MEET?

MAR 5

DON'T WORRY ABOUT FAILING.

PEOPLE ALREADY KNOW YOU WILL FAIL.

MAR 6

FOLLOW THE ADVICE OF THAT INTERNET GURU.

BUY THAT COURSE ON HOW TO BECOME A BROKER.

MAR 7

YOU DON'T NEED ADVICE.

YOU KNOW HOW TO MAKE MISTAKES ON YOUR OWN.

MAR 8

THE BEST WAY TO DEAL WITH PROBLEMS IS TO ADD NEW PROBLEMS SO YOU FORGET ABOUT THE OTHERS.

MAR 9

YOU MAY THINK THAT TODAY WAS NOT YOUR LUCKY DAY.

BUT NEITHER WILL IT BE TOMORROW.

MAR 10

FOCUS ON YOUR GOAL.

AND NOW RELAX BECAUSE YOU WILL NEVER REACH IT.

MAR 11

ASK FOR ADVICE IS FOR LOSERS.

MAR 12

RELAX YOU COULDN'T HAVE KNOWN.

BUT EVEN IF YOU HAD KNOWN, YOU WOULDN'T HAVE DONE ANY BETTER.

MAR 13

LOOK AT THE PEOPLE AROUND YOU.

THEY ARE DOING WELL.

MAR 14

TODAY IT'S " P " DAY.

WHERE " P " STANDS FOR PAIN.

MAR 15

LOWER YOUR STANDARDS.

MAR 16

SUCCESS IS LIKE A RARE UNICORN - DIFFICULT TO FIND, AND PROBABLY MYTHICAL.

MAR 17

THE ONLY THING WORSE THAN FAILING IS TRYING, SO WHY BOTHER?

MAR 18

DREAM BIG, BUT PREPARE FOR EVEN BIGGER DISAPPOINTMENTS.

MAR 19

YOU SHOULD DO MORE.

BUT NOT TODAY.

MAR 20

DON'T GIVE UP.

KEEP DOING WHAT YOU DO.

PEOPLE LAUGH AT YOU WHEN YOU FAIL.

KEEP MAKING THEM LAUGH.

MAR 21

FEEL DISAPPOINTED?

YOU'D BETTER.

MAR 22

DON'T DO IT FOR YOURSELF.

DO IT TO PLEASE OTHERS.

MAR 23

DON'T TAKE A POSITION, DON'T TAKE SIDES.

MAR 24

NOT TRYING IS BETTER THAN TRYING AND FAILING.

MAR 25

DO YOU KNOW WHAT YOU SHOULD DO?

NOTHING.

MAR 26

DOING A GOOD DEED IS AN ACT OF WEAKNESS.

ONLY LOSERS ARE SELFLESS.

MAR 27

THERE ARE TWO RULES IN LIFE:

1) NEVER FOLLOW YOUR DREAMS.

2) NEVER FORGET RULE NUMBER 1.

MAR 28

AMBITION IS THE FIRST STEP ON THE PATH TO OVERCOMMITMENT AND EXHAUSTION.

MAR 29

IT'S NEVER TOO LATE

TO MAKE THE BIGGEST FAILURE OF YOUR LIFE.

MAR 30

CAREER ADVANCEMENT IS LIKE A LEPRECHAUN - RARELY SEEN AND PROBABLY IMAGINARY.

MAR 31

SPORT IT'S ONLY USEFUL TO CONSUME THAT LITTLE ENERGY LEFTOVER AFTER AN EXHAUSTING WORKING DAY.

APR 1

LIFE IS THE REAL APRIL 'S FOOL.

APR 2

IF YOU DON'T BELIEVE IN YOURSELF, AT LEAST, YOU ARE DOING SOMETHING RIGHT.

APR 3

MOUNTAINS ARE MADE TO BE CLIMBED.

BY OTHERS.

APR 4

**WORK HARD, THEY SAID.
IT'LL PAY OFF, THEY SAID.**

THEY LIED.

APR 5

MAKE NO EFFORT.

STOP AT THE FIRST OBSTACLE.

APR 6

LET THE FEAR OF MAKING MISTAKES OVERWHELM YOU.

APR 7

NO MATTER HOW FAST YOU GO.

YOU WILL STILL ALWAYS ARRIVE LATER THAN OTHERS.

APR 8

IF IT GOES WRONG THE FIRST TIME, THERE IS NO POINT IN CONTINUING TO TRY.

APR 9

SUCCESS IS DEFINITIVE.

FAILURE IS FATAL.

APR 10

DON'T CARPE THAT DIEM.

APR 11

OPPORTUNITIES COME AND GO.

FOR OTHERS OF COURSE.

NOT FOR YOU.

APR 12

YOU CANNOT DO ANYTHING AGAINST INJUSTICE.

YOU CAN ONLY STAND STILL AND SUFFER IT.

APR 13

SURRENDER TODAY.

THAT TOMORROW MAY BE THE LUCKY DAY WHEN YOU MAKE IT.

APR 14

NEVER MAKE YOUR OWN CONTRIBUTION.

APR 15

MAKE UP EXCUSES TO CONVINCE YOURSELF THAT YOU ARE NOT WASTING YOUR TIME.

APR 16

ENVY OTHERS.

APR 17

SUCCESS IS FOR THE FEW.

YOU ARE NOT AMONG THEM.

APR 18

AVOID INTERESTING PEOPLE.

THEY MIGHT GIVE YOU GOOD IDEAS.

APR 19

NO ONE EXPECTS ANYTHING FROM YOU.

APR 20

TO KEEP HOPING IS JUST A WAY TO KEEP DELUDING YOURSELF.

APR 21

YOU CAN'T CHANGE THINGS.

APR 22

DON'T STOP WHEN YOU ARE TIRED.

STOP WHEN YOU HAVE FAILED.

APR 23

DON'T FOCUS.

DISTRACT YOURSELF.

WASTE TIME.

APR 24

REMINDER:

IF YOU FALL, DON'T GET BACK UP.

APR 25

NO PAIN, NO PAIN. SKIP THE GYM, FEEL NO PAIN.

APR 26

THE FACT THAT YOU CAN DO IT DOESN'T MEAN THAT YOU HAVE TO TRY.

APR 27

LET YOURSELF BE INTIMIDATED BY CHALLENGES THAT SEEM DIFFICULT.

APR 28

YOU MAY BE GOOD AT SOMETHING.

BUT THERE WILL ALWAYS BE SOMEONE BETTER THAN YOU.

APR 29

IF YOU BELIEVE IT, YOU ARE ALREADY FAILING.

APR 30

EVEN THE GREATEST FAIL.

YOU FAIL AND YOU ARE NOT EVEN AMONG THE GREATEST.

MAY 1

MAY 2

YOU DON'T LIKE YOURSELF?

IF IT'S ANY CONSOLATION, OTHER PEOPLE DON'T LIKE YOU EITHER.

MAY 3

STOP AS SOON AS YOU ARE
A LITTLE TIRED.

DON'T BELIEVE YOU CAN
DO IT.

MAY 4

DON'T EXPECT ANYTHING FROM PEOPLE.

WHY SHOULD THEY TRUST YOU?

MAY 5

IF IT REQUIRES EFFORT.

AVOID IT.

MAY 6

TODAY'S TASK:

DO NOT ACHIEVE ANY GOALS.

MAY 7

FAKE IT.

'CAUSE YOU WON'T MAKE IT.

MAY 8

YOU SHOULD HAVE THOUGHT OF THIS YEARS AGO; NOW IT IS TOO LATE.

MAY 9

DO YOU DREAM OF BECOMING RICH?

GO BACK TO BED AND KEEP DREAMING.

MAY 10

BODY NEGATIVITY IS THE KEY.

MAY 11

LOOK IN THE MIRROR.

NOW YOU SEE THE PROBLEM.

MAY 12

CHASING YOUR DREAMS IS A WASTE OF TIME.

MAY 13

LISTEN TO THOSE WHO TELL YOU TO GIVE UP.

MAY 14

BE AFRAID OF THE FUTURE, RESPONSIBILITIES WILL GROW DAY BY DAY.

MAY 15

BELIEVING IN YOURSELF IS THE FIRST MISTAKE.

TRYING HARD IS THE SECOND.

MAY 16

IT'S ALL ABOUT THE MINDSET.

A MINDSET YOU DON'T HAVE.

MAY 17

ARE YOU SURE YOU WANT TO RISK IT?

SPARE YOURSELF THIS ADDITIONAL SHAME.

BE KIND TO YOURSELF.

MAY 18

THE WORLD BELONGS TO THOSE WHO DREAM BIG.

GO BACK TO BED AND KEEP DREAMING.

MAY 19

DO YOU REMEMBER WHEN YOU WERE A CHILD AND YOU WANTED TO BE FAMOUS WHEN YOU GREW UP?

YOU FAILED.

MAY 20

DO YOU REMEMBER THAT HOUSE OF YOUR DREAMS?

A GUY RICHER THAN YOU JUST BOUGHT IT.

MAY 21

IF YOU ARE READING THIS, IT'S TOO LATE.

GIVE UP.

MAY 22

LOOK ON THE BRIGHT SIDE:

NO ONE WILL EVER STEAL YOUR FERRARI.

MAY 23

ALWAYS REMEMBER TO GIVE BIRTHDAY WISHES TO YOUR FRIENDS.

THEY WILL BE THE ONES TO LEND YOU MONEY WHEN YOU ARE BROKE.

MAY 24.

YOU ARE JUST BELOW AVERAGE.

MAY 25

WHY MAKE PLANS WHEN YOU CAN JUST WING IT AND FAIL?

MAY 26

DO YOU REMEMBER THAT JOB YOU SO ASPIRED TO?

SOMEONE ELSE WAS HIRED INSTEAD OF YOU.

MAY 27

IT IS NOT YOUR FAULT IF YOU ARE NOT ATTRACTIVE.

BUT THERE'S NOTHING YOU CAN DO ABOUT IT.

JUST ACCEPT IT.

MAY 28

DON'T BE AFRAID TO FIGHT FOR WHAT YOU BELIEVE IN.

BE AFRAID OF FAILING. THAT ALWAYS HURTS.

MAY 29

IF YOU FAIL

GET BACK UP.

SO YOU CAN FAIL AGAIN.

MAY 30

IF THEY ASK YOU HOW YOU ARE DOING, DON'T BE HONEST.

SAY THAT YOU ARE DOING WELL.

MAY 31

NO.

REPLYING AT THAT E MAIL IS NOT A HUGE ACCOMPLISHMENT.

JUN 1

DO YOU REALLY WANT TO STOP FAILING?

FAILING

BECAUSE YOU ARE REALLY GOOD AT THIS.

JUN 2

ROME WAS NOT BUILT IN A DAY.

BUT AT LEAST IT WAS BUILT.

JUN 3

You came,

You saw,

You came back to where you were from.

JUN 4

IF YOU REALLY BELIEVE THAT YOU CAN DO IT,

THEN YOU'RE WRONG.

JUN 5

FAILURE IS ALWAYS AN OPTION.

CONSIDER IT.

JUN 6

IS NOT ABOUT OTHERS.

IT'S ABOUT YOU.

IT'S YOUR LIFE THAT IS A MESS.

JUN 7

DON'T BE ASHAMED TO BE WEAK.

WEAKNESS IS YOUR ONLY QUALITY.

BE PROUD OF IT.

JUN 8

HARD WORK MAY PAY OFF IN THE FUTURE, BUT LAZINESS PAYS OFF RIGHT NOW.

JUN 9

IT'S NOT TOO COMPLICATED.

IT'S JUST THAT YOU CAN'T DO IT.

JUN 10

I'M SORRY TO POINT THIS OUT, BUT TIME IS PASSING FAST.

WHAT HAVE BEEN YOUR ACHIEVEMENTS SO FAR?

JUN 11

THE MORE YOU EXPECT, THE MORE YOU'LL BE LET DOWN.

JUN 12

SUCCESS IS AN ILLUSION.

JUN 13

DON'T CRY.

IT WON'T HELP.

OR MAYBE IT WILL.

JUN 14

SMILE.

NOW GO TO WORK.

YOUR BOSS NEEDS TO YELL
AT SOMEONE'S FACE.

JUN 15

PEOPLE CAN BE RUDE SOMETIMES.

BUT HOW CAN YOU BLAME THEM?

JUN 16

REMEMBER TO POST THAT ONE PICTURE WHERE YOU LOOK HAPPY.

PEOPLE WILL THINK YOU REALLY ARE.

JUN 17

LOOK AT THE BRIGHT SIDE:

IT COULD HARDLY GET ANY WORSE THAN THIS.

JUN 18

PRETEND TO BE HAPPY.

IT'S THE BEST YOU CAN DO.

JUN 19

MONEY WON'T MAKE YOU HAPPY.

PAYING YOUR RENT WILL.

JUN 20

STOP THINKING THAT YOU CAN MAKE A DIFFERENCE.

IT'S NOT 2009 ANYMORE.

THERE'S NOTHING MORE YOU CAN DO.

JUN 21

TODAY IS A GOOD DAY TO FAIL.

JUN 22

IT'S NEVER TOO LATE TO GIVE UP.

JUN 23

STEVE JOBS FOUNDED APPLE AT AGE 22.

IT'S TOO LATE.

GIVE UP.

JUN 24

WHAT YOU COULD DO IS STOP DREAMING.

YOU CAN'T BREAK YOUR DREAMS IF YOU DON'T HAVE DREAMS.

JUN 25

LIFE-CHANGING OPPORTUNITIES EXIST.

AND YOU MISS THEM ALL.

JUN 26

INSUCCESS IS THE SUM OF SMALL EFFORTS REPEATED DAY AFTER DAY.

JUN 27

THE ONLY THING GUARANTEED IN THE FUTURE IS UNCERTAINTY.

JUN 28

THE BEGINNING IS THE MOST IMPORTANT PART OF A JOB.

SO DON'T EVEN START.

JUN 29

BE GUIDED BY FEAR.

IS THE BEST WAY TO MAKE BAD DECISIONS.

JUN 30

YOU WILL NEVER FAIL AS LONG AS YOU KEEP TRYING.

SO, STOP TRYING.

JUL 1

JUST DON' T DO IT.

JUL 2

LOOK AWAY FROM YOUR GOAL.

YOU KNOW VERY WELL THAT IT IS UNACHIEVABLE.

JUL 3

CHALLENGES ARE WHAT MAKE LIFE INTERESTING.

DO YOU REALLY WANT AN INTERESTING LIFE?

A BORING ONE IS WAY BETTER.

JUL 4

ALWAYS DEVOTE LITTLE TIME TO YOURSELF.

SAVE ENERGY FOR YOUR JOB.

JUL 5

YOU DESERVE A VACATION.

BUT NOT TODAY.

TODAY YOU HAVE TO WORK.

JUL 6

DON'T TRY TO CHANGE THE WORLD.

SOMEONE ELSE BETTER THAN YOU WILL.

YOU DON'T HAVE TO WORRY ABOUT IT.

JUL 7

YOUR DREAMS OF WEALTH WILL BE PERFECTLY PRESERVED IN YOUR IMAGINATION.

JUL 8

THEY SAY THE SKY'S THE LIMIT, BUT YOU SHOULD BE COMFORTABLE STAYING GROUNDED.

JUL 9

ONLY MONEY CAN BUY YOU HAPPINESS.

JUL 10

GO AHEAD AND BLAME SOCIETY IF THAT MAKES YOU FEEL BETTER.

JUL 11

NO MATTER HOW MANY TIMES YOU FAIL.

IT'S HOW YOU FAIL THAT'S FUNNY.

JUL 12

AIMS HIGHER AND HIGHER.

SO FALLING WILL ALWAYS HURT MORE AND MORE.

JUL 13

KEEP IT UP.

IN THE END, DEDICATING YOUR LIFE TO YOUR WORK IS NOT THAT BAD.

JUL 14

DO YOU REMEMBER THE LAST TIME YOU WERE HAPPY?

THEN YOU HAVE A GOOD MEMORY.

JUL 15

YOU ARE NOT A HERO IF YOU RECYCLE PLASTIC BOTTLES.

YOU WON'T SAVE THE PLANET.

JUL 16

YOU DESERVE MORE.

BUT STILL, YOU WILL DO NOTHING TO CHANGE THINGS.

JUL 17

LIST YOUR WEAK POINTS.

THIS OPERATION SHOULD KEEP YOU BUSY FOR QUITE SOME TIME.

JUL 18

DON'T WORKOUT.
IT'S USELESS.

JUL 19

DON'T WORRY ABOUT THAT MISSED OPPORTUNITY.

YOU WILL MISS MANY MORE.

JUL 20

WORRY MORE ABOUT INSIGNIFICANT THINGS.

JUL 21

WHY DO YOU HATE THE WHOLE WORLD?

PEOPLE DON'T EVEN KNOW YOU EXIST.

JUL 22

SEE HOW HAPPY PEOPLE ARE ON SOCIAL MEDIA.

JUL 23

NO, TODAY IS NOT THE DAY YOU WILL CHANGE THE WORLD.

GO BACK TO SLEEP.

# JUL 24

EXPECTATIONS ARE JUST PREMEDITATED RESENTMENTS..

JUL 25

I KNOW YOU WOULD LIKE TO CHANGE YOUR LIFE.

BUT DON'T THINK ABOUT IT NOW, YOU'LL DO IT LATER.

JUL 26

SUMMER IS MAGIC.

FOR THE OTHERS.

JUL 27

IT IS ALL MUCH MORE DIFFICULT THAN IT SEEMS.

JUL 28

THE BEST WAY TO AVOID DISAPPOINTMENT IN RELATIONSHIPS IS TO HAVE NONE.

JUL 29

FEEL FREE TO EXPRESS YOUR IDEAS.

BUT DON'T EXPECT ANYONE TO CARE ABOUT WHAT YOU HAVE TO SAY.

JUL 30

AVOID SEROTONIN.

JUL 31

TODAY IS A GOOD DAY TO GO TO THE SEA AND ENJOY SUMMER.

GOOD.

NOW GO TO WORK.

AUG 1

MAKE SURE YOU ALWAYS DO LESS THAN YOU COULD DO.

AUG 2

NEVER COMPLETE A TASK.

AND IF YOU MUST,
COMPLETE IT LATE.

AUG 3

DON'T LEARN NEW SKILLS.

THE FEW YOU HAVE ARE ENOUGH TO FAIL.

AUG 4

DO YOU EVER THINK ABOUT WHAT YOU WILL BE LIKE IN 10 YEARS?

YOU'D BETTER NOT.

AUG 5

THE BEST WAY TO AVOID DISAPPOINTMENT IS TO AVOID PEOPLE.

AUG 6

SUCCESS ARISES WHERE LUCK AND HARD WORK MEET.

KEEP THESE TWO THINGS TRAVEL ON PARALLEL LINES.

AUG 7

REMEMBER:

IF YOU DECIDE TO DO SOMETHING, DO IT WRONG, OR DON'T DO IT AT ALL.

AUG 8

ALWAYS TRY NOT TO LEARN ANYTHING FROM YOUR MISTAKES.

SO THAT YOU CAN KEEP FAILING IN THE SAME COMFORTABLE WAY.

AUG 9

SLEEP LESS THAN 4 HOURS PER NIGHT.

DRINK COFFEE.

EAT POORLY.

AUG 10

NEVER MAKE THE MOST OF YOUR POTENTIAL.

AUG 11

ALWAYS TRY TO COMPARE YOURSELF WITH OTHERS.

IT WILL MAKE YOU REMEMBER HOW FAR YOU ARE FROM YOUR GOAL AND MAKE YOU GIVE UP.

AUG 12

THE GREAT THING ABOUT TEAMWORK IS THAT YOU ARE ALLOWED TO DO NOTHING.

AUG 13

IF YOU WANT TO BE A LEADER, THINK AGAIN.

YOU ARE NOT MADE FOR THIS.

AUG 14

TRYING TO REALIZE YOUR DREAMS IS THE BEST WAY TO WASTE TIME.

AUG 15

MAKE THE PEOPLE AROUND YOU DISRESPECT YOU.

AUG 16

NO MATTER HOW MANY TIMES YOU TRY.

YOU WILL ALWAYS FAIL.

AUG 17

IF YOU BELIEVE IN YOURSELF, YOU ARE ALREADY DOING WRONG.

AUG 18

DO NOT GET THE JOB DONE.

MAKE UP AN EXCUSE.

DON'T ACHIEVE THE RESULTS.

AUG 19

ONCE YOU START TO FAIL ON A REGULAR BASIS, THE HARD PART IS TO STOP.

AUG 20

YOU MISS ONE HUNDRED PERCENT OF THE SHOTS YOU TAKE.

AUG 21

IF SOMETHING STANDS BETWEEN YOU AND YOUR SUCCESS, LEAVE IT THERE, DON'T MOVE IT.

AUG 22

NEVER, AND I SAY NEVER, LEAVE YOUR COMFORT ZONE.

AUG 23

LET FAILURE BECOME A HABIT.

AUG 24

NEVER LOOK FOR MOTIVATION TO DO SOMETHING.

COMPLAINING IS THE BEST PRACTICE.

AUG 25

DON'T EXPECT ANYTHING FROM YOURSELF.

AUG 26

WHEN YOU HAVE A CLEAR VISION OF YOUR GOALS, IT IS EASIER TO FAIL IN THE RIGHT WAY.

AUG 27

When you feel tired, give up, it's over, go back to bed.

You'll try again another day.

AUG 28

TODAY YOU WOKE UP TO BE MORE MEDIOCRE THAN YESTERDAY AND LESS MEDIOCRE THAN TOMORROW.

AUG 29

WE CAN PUSH OURSELVES FURTHER.

BUT THERE IS NO REASON TO DO SO.

AUG 30

DON'T DREAM OF WINNING.

THERE IS NO POINT IN DOING SO.

AUG 31

LISTEN TO YOUR BODY.

IS TELLING YOU TO GIVE UP.

SEP 1

THE ODDS ARE AGAINST YOU.

SEP 2

IF YOU THINK YOU CAN'T DO IT, YOU'RE RIGHT.

YOU CAN'T DO IT.

SEP 3

PUT ALL EXCUSES ASIDE AND REMEMBER THIS:

YOU ARE NOT CAPABLE.

SEP 4

YOU ARE NOT ENOUGH.

SEP 5

GIVE YOURSELF A BREAK, YOU DESERVE IT FOR DOING NOTHING.

SEP 6

THINGS DON'T WORK OUT FOR A REASON.

THE REASON IS YOU.

SEP 7

YOU SHOULD WORRY A LITTLE BIT MORE ABOUT WHAT PEOPLE THINK OF YOU.

THEY'RE JUDGING YOU.

SEP 8

DON'T TELL OTHERS ABOUT YOUR PROBLEMS.

YOU WOULD LOOK LIKE A WEIRDO.

SEP 9

GIVING UP IT'S THE EASIER WAY.

TAKE IT.

SEP 10

DISAPPOINTED WITH YOUR LIFE?

GET USED TO IT.

SEP 11

LOWER YOUR EXPECTATIONS.

SEP 12

DON'T DO ANYTHING PRODUCTIVE TODAY.

SEP 13

BE AFRAID TO FAIL.

IT IS AN EMBARRASSING THING.

OTHERS WILL LAUGH AT YOU.

SEP 14

IT'S TOO LATE TO CHANGE YOUR LIFE.

YOU SHOULD HAVE THOUGHT ABOUT IT BEFORE.

SEP 15

STOP BELIEVING IN YOURSELF.

IT'S TOO LATE NOW.

IT DOESN'T MAKE SENSE ANYMORE.

SEP 16

IT'S ALWAYS A GOOD DAY TO MAKE BAD DECISIONS.

SEP 17

IT'S OBVIOUS THAT IT'S YOUR FAULT.

WHOSE ELSE COULD IT BE?

SEP 18

FIND AN EXCUSE TODAY AS WELL.

BECAUSE YOU WILL NOT MAKE ANY ACCOMPLISHMENT.

SEP 19

WORK LIFE BALANCE IS A MYTH.

IT JUST DOESN'T EXIST.

ACCEPT IT.

SEP 20

OPTIMISM IS WHAT WILL RUIN YOU.

BE REALISTIC.

SEP 21

DON'T THINK YOU ARE
BETTER THAN OTHERS.

YOU ARE NOT.

SEP 22

PEOPLE SAY NOTHING IS IMPOSSIBLE.

PEOPLE ARE WRONG.

SEP 23

JUST ONE SMALL NEGATIVE THOUGHT IN THE MORNING CAN CHANGE YOUR WHOLE DAY.

THINK NEGATIVE.

SEP 24

MAKE PEOPLE FEEL UNCOMFORTABLE AROUND YOU.

SEP 25

IT IS TOO LATE TO BE WHAT YOU MIGHT HAVE BEEN.

GIVE UP.

SEP 26

DO YOUR BEST.

THERE WILL ALWAYS BE SOMEONE BETTER THAN YOU ANYWAY.

SEP 27

BE MISERABLE.

SEP 28

IF YOU REALLY WANT SOMETHING TO HAPPEN, FIND AN EXCUSE NOT TO MAKE IT HAPPEN.

SEP 29

COURAGE IS THE LESS IMPORTANT OF ALL THE VIRTUES.

YOU DON'T NEED IT.

SEP 30

EVERYTHING YOU EVER DREAMED OF, BECOMES MORE UNATTAINABLE EVERY DAY.

OCT 1

YOU COULD HAVE BEEN ANYTHING.

OR MAYBE NOT.

OR MAYBE NOT!

OCT 2

FOR OTHERS LIFE SEEMS EASY.

IT'S BECAUSE IT IS.

IT'S YOU WHO CAN'T HANDLE IT.

OCT 3

FOCUS LESS ON THE WORK TO BE DONE.

GIVE YOURSELF LONG BREAKS.

WASTE TIME.

OCT 4

LOWER YOUR GAZE.

WALK WITH YOUR HEAD DOWN.

BE ASHAMED, ALWAYS.

OCT 5

IDENTIFY YOUR ENEMY

AND THEN RUN AWAY.

DON'T FACE IT.

IT'S STRONGER THAN YOU.

OCT 6

IF YOUR GREATEST FEAR IS TO FAIL, THEN THIS FEAR IS WELL-FOUNDED.

OCT 7

IF YOU FEEL THE NEED TO SAY SOMETHING.

DON'T SAY IT.

IT MAY BE SOMETHING STUPID.

OCT 8

GO TO BED UNSATISFIED.

TOMORROW WILL BE WORSE.

OCT 9

CONCENTRATE YOUR ENERGY ON MANY UNCOORDINATED AND DISJOINTED IDEAS.

OCT 10

WE GENERATE FEARS WHILE WE SIT.

WE OVERCOME THEM BY ACTION.

DON'T ACT, ENJOY YOUR FEARS.

OCT 11

YOU DON'T NEED TO TAKE RISKS.

YOU DON'T NEED TO PROVE THEM WRONG.

YOU DON'T NEED TO CHANGE THE SYSTEM.

OCT 12

EMBRACE CAPITALISM.

NOW GO AND SATISFY YOUR BOSS.

OCT 13

IF YOU ARE LOOKING FOR A HAPPY LIFE.

STOP LOOKING FOR IT.

OCT 14

A LOT OF PEOPLE ARE AFRAID TO SAY WHAT THEY WANT.

YOU ARE ONE OF THEM,

LUCKLY.

OCT 15

"BEING VULNERABLE IS A STRENGTH, NOT A WEAKNESS."

IS WHAT LOSERS SAY.

OCT 16

THERE IS ALWAYS LIGHT.

IF ONLY YOU' RE BRAVE ENOUGH TO SEE IT.

BUT YOU' RE NOT.

OCT 17

IF YOU WANT TO LIFT YOURSELF UP, CHANGE YOUR PLANS.

NOT TODAY CHAMP.

OCT 18

YOU'RE BRAVER THAN YOU BELIEVE, STRONGER THAN YOU SEEM, AND SMARTER THAN YOU THINK...

...AND OTHER LIES YOU TELL YOURSELF.

OCT 19

WHEN YOU FEEL LIKE QUITTING, QUIT.

OCT 20

DO NOT EMBARK ON THIS NEW ADVENTURE.

IT MAY BE RISKY.

YOU MAY FAIL AGAIN.

OCT 21

DID YOU GET THAT GYM MEMBERSHIP YOU WERE TALKING ABOUT IN JANUARY?

OCT 22

THE KEY THING IS TO LOSE HOPE.

OCT 23

THE WORST IS YET TO COME.

OCT 24

OF COURSE MONEY IS NOT IMPORTANT.

BUT I DON'T THINK YOU CAN PAY THE RENT WITH TEARS.

OCT 25

BE SATISFIED WITH A MEDIOCRE LIFE.

OCT 26

BEING DESPERATE DOESN'T HELP.

BUT WHAT ELSE COULD YOU DO?

OCT 27

NO ONE WARNED YOU THAT LIFE WOULD BE SO DIFFICULT.

OTHERS WERE WARNED, BUT YOU WERE NOT.

OCT 28

REPLACE POSITIVE THOUGHTS WITH NEGATIVE ONES.

OCT 29

KEEP WASTING YOUR TIME.

OCT 30

TAKE INSPIRATION FROM PEOPLE WHO HAVE NO AMBITION.

OCT 31

DO NOT DIVERSIFY YOUR INVESTMENTS.

MISMANAGE YOUR MONEY.

SPEND MORE THAN WHAT YOU EARN.

NOV 1

COME ON, MAKE AN HR LAUGH.

fa[in]ng

APPLY FOR THAT POSITION.

NOV 2

JOB SATISFACTION IS LIKE BIGFOOT. EVERYONE TALKS ABOUT IT, BUT NO ONE HAS SEEN IT.

NOV 3

IT IS DIFFICULT TO GET
USED TO CHANGE.

DON' T CHANGE.

NOV 4

YOUR TIME IS NOT SO PRECIOUS.

MONEY IS.

NOV 5

COMPLETE THE EASY TASKS FIRST, WHEN YOU ARE FULL OF ENERGY.

LEAVE THE HARD ONES FOR LATER, WHEN YOU ARE TIRED.

NOV 6

IF PEOPLE DON'T BELIEVE IN YOU, DON'T GIVE THEM A REASON TO.

NOV 7

TO LOVE SOMEONE IS FOR WEAK PEOPLE.

NOV 8

DON'T LEAVE THE BAD MEMORIES BEHIND.

EVERY ONCE IN A WHILE, REMEMBER THEM AND FEEL BAD.

NOV 9

REMEMBER THAT A DEFEAT ALWAYS HURTS A LOT.

IT IS BETTER NOT TO FIGHT AND NOT EVEN TRY TO WIN.

NOV 10

IF YOU STILL HAVE A SHRED OF ENTHUSIASM, LEAVE IT BEHIND.

IT' S USELESS.

NOV 11

THERE IS NO REASON TO BE HAPPY.

NOV 12

DON'T GO BEYOND YOUR LIMITS.

YOU KNOW VERY WELL YOU CAN'T DO THAT.

IT WOULD ONLY HURT.

NOV 13

LET THE FEAR OF MAKING A MISTAKE OVERCOME THE EXCITEMENT OF VICTORY.

NOV 14

EVERYONE FAILS.

THIS IS WHAT LOSERS LIKE TO BELIEVE.

NOV 15

BE TAMED AND SUBDUED BY ADVERSITY.

DON'T GET BACK UP.

NOV 16

YOUR TIME ON THIS PLANET IS LIMITED.

USE IT TO PLEASE YOUR BOSS.

NOV 17

TRY NEVER TO BE CLEAR ABOUT YOUR GOAL.

NOV 18

WAIT A LITTLE LONGER TO START THAT PROJECT YOU LIKE.

THERE'S STILL PLENTY OF TIME.

GO TO WORK TODAY.

NOV 19

DON'T LISTEN TO OTHER PEOPLE'S OPINIONS.

NEVER QUESTION YOURSELF.

BELIEVE EVERYTHING YOU ARE TOLD.

NOV 20

DO NOTHING.

SO YOU WON'T MAKE MISTAKES AND NO ONE WILL LAUGH AT YOU.

NOV 21

A GOOD DIET AND A LOT OF WILLPOWER WILL NOT GET YOU THE PERFECT BODY YOU DESIRE.

YOU NEED MOTHER NATURE FOR THAT.

NOV 22

DON'T BE CURIOUS.

DON'T ASK QUESTIONS.

ACCEPT THE WORLD FOR WHAT IT IS.

NOV 23

NEVER BE CONFIDENT.

NOV 24

DON'T SHOW YOURSELF TO OTHERS AS YOU REALLY ARE.

NO ONE CARES.

NOV 25

You must not have the strength to face the most difficult situations.

Let small obstacles stop you, don't try to overcome them.

NOV 26

IT IS NOT TRUE THAT THE ONLY LIMITS ARE THOSE YOU SET FOR YOURSELF.

SOME LIMITS ARE SET BY OTHERS, AND THEY ARE INSURMOUNTABLE.

NOV 27

ACCEPT INJUSTICES FOR WHAT THEY ARE AND SUFFER THE CONSEQUENCES.

NOV 28

DON'T BE ALTRUISTIC.

DON'T HELP OTHERS.

THE WORLD IS BAD.

BE BAD.

NOV 29

IF YOU ARE LOOKING FOR WILLPOWER IN YOURSELF,

THEN YOU ARE LOOKING IN THE WRONG PLACE.

NOV 30

THINK BACK TO THE MISTAKES YOU HAVE MADE IN THE PAST AND MAKE THEM AGAIN.

DEC 1

HAVE THE STRENGTH TO STOP BELIEVING IN YOUR DREAMS AND ACCEPT THE MEDIOCRE LIFE YOU ARE LIVING.

DEC 2

SURROUND YOURSELF WITH PEOPLE WHO MAKE YOU FEEL WORTHLESS.

DEC 3

FIND A JOB THAT DOES NOT STIMULATE YOUR CREATIVITY.

EVEN BETTER IF IT IS DEPRESSING.

DEC 4

ALWAYS TRUST FAKE NEWS.

DO NOT INFORM YOURSELF.

DEC 5

YOU DON'T HAVE TO FACE THE PROBLEMS.

LET THEM SOLVE THEMSELVES OR LET SOMEONE SOLVE THEM FOR YOU.

DEC 6

GETTING UP AFTER A DEFEAT ONLY MAKES YOU MORE RIDICULOUS.

DEC 7

IF YOU HAVE FAILED ONCE,
YOU WILL ALWAYS FAIL.

FOREVER.

DEC 8

LIFE IS JUST A MATTER OF LUCK. COMMITMENT HAS NOTHING TO DO WITH IT.

ONLY THE LUCKY MAKE IT, NOT THOSE WHO WORK HARD TO MAKE IT.

DEC 9

THE WORLD IS UNFAIR AND YOU CAN'T DO ANYTHING TO CHANGE IT.

JUST ACCEPT IT.

DEC 10

IF YOU'RE GOOD AT SOMETHING, DON'T DO IT.

DEC 11

DO NOT EXPRESS YOUR
POTENTIAL.

DEC 12

DON'T SPEND TIME ON THE PEOPLE YOU LOVE.

USE IT TO DO UNNECESSARY AND DEGRADING THINGS INSTEAD.

DEC 13

FOCUS ON WHAT MAKES YOU FEEL BAD.

DEC 14

LIFE IS FULL OF OPPORTUNITIES.

AVOID THEM.

DEC 15

DON'T TAKE ADVICE FROM ANYONE.

DON'T LET THOSE WHO HAVE MORE EXPERIENCE THAN YOU GIVE YOU A HAND.

DEC 16

TRUST THE WRONG PEOPLE.

ALWAYS.

DEC 17

THE REAL DEFEAT LIES IN HAVING EVEN TRIED.

DEC 18

DON'T TRY TO FIGURE OUT WHERE YOU'RE GOING WRONG.

FIND JUSTIFICATIONS TO CONVINCE YOURSELF THAT YOU ARE NOT GOING WRONG INSTEAD.

DEC 19

NEVER QUESTION YOUR OWN OPINIONS.

IF YOU BELIEVE ONE THING IT WILL SURELY BE THAT WAY.

DON'T LISTEN TO OTHER PEOPLE'S OPINIONS ABOUT IT.

DEC 20

TAKES ADVICE FROM THE WRONG PEOPLE.

DEC 21

DON'T LISTEN TO THOSE WHO WANT TO HELP YOU.

DEC 22

SPEND YOUR FREE TIME ON SOCIAL MEDIA.

AVOID EXHIBITIONS, MUSEUMS, CONCERTS AND SHOWS.

ALWAYS AVOID GOING OUTDOORS.

DEC 23

FOLLOW THE CROWD.

DO WHAT EVERYONE DOES.

DON'T THINK OUTSIDE THE BOX.

DEC 24

DON'T THINK YOU'RE SPECIAL.

DON'T DELUDE YOURSELF.

DEC 25

SANTA CLAUS DOES NOT EXIST.

DEC 26

DON'T LET THE GOOD TIMES DISTRACT YOU FROM THE MISTAKES YOU'VE MADE IN THE PAST.

DEC 27

BELIEVING IN SOMETHING IS THE FIRST STEP TO FAILING MISERABLY.

DEC 28

STILL NO PLANS FOR NEW YEAR'S EVE?

DEC 29

DON'T THINK THAT FAILING CAN TEACH YOU ANYTHING.

IT ONLY MAKES YOU MORE RIDICULOUS IN THE EYES OF OTHERS.

DEC 30

HOPE IS THE FIRST STEP ON THE ROAD TO CRUSHING DISAPPOINTMENT.

DEC 31

DON'T LET A NEW BEGINNING SPUR YOU ON TO ACCOMPLISH SOMETHING GREAT.

AIN'T NOTHING CHANGES.

EVERYTHING REMAINS AS IT ALWAYS HAS BEEN AND AS IT ALWAYS WILL BE.

THE END.

TOMORROW YOU CAN START AGAIN FROM THE BEGINNING.

Printed in Great Britain
by Amazon